I0763961

ASK DR. LINQ LLC
PUBLISHING · MEDIA · COUNSELING

WHY HE HASN'T MARRIED YOU

The Truth About Male Commitment and Intentional Dating

MANUEL V. JOHNSON

WHY HE HASN'T MARRIED YOU

Published by: Manuel Johnson | Ask Dr. Linq, LLC.

Ask Dr. Linq Book Collection

ISBN: 979-8-9938638-1-8

Printed in United States of America
First Edition: February 2026

www.AskDrLinq.com

For permissions requests, contact:
AskDrLinqInfo@gmail.com

The information provided in this book, *Why He Hasn't Married You*, is for general informational and educational purposes only. The content reflects the author's research, observations, experiences, and personal viewpoints on relationships, dating, and human behavior.

This book is not intended to replace professional counseling, therapy, legal advice, or any other form of professional guidance. Relationship situations vary from person to person, and readers are encouraged to use their own judgment when applying any insights discussed in this book.

The author and publisher make no guarantees regarding specific outcomes or results. Any actions taken based on the information in this book are done at the reader's own discretion and responsibility.

By reading this book, you acknowledge that you are responsible for your own decisions, emotional wellbeing, and relationship choices. The author and publisher are not liable for any emotional, relational, or personal outcomes that may result from the use or interpretation of the material presented.

DISCLAIMER FOR MEN

If this book causes your woman to start asking real questions, rethinking her situation, or deciding she no longer wants to wait around, do not come looking for me. I did not break up your relationship. I did not tell her to leave you. I did not make your situation what it is. I simply wrote down things that were already happening. Whatever choices she makes after reading this are her choices, just like whatever choices she made before this book were hers. If you truly want her, marry her. If you do not, be honest with her. Either way, the outcome belongs to the two of you, not this book and not me.

TABLE OF CONTENTS

INTRODUCTION

If you are reading this book, you are likely not new to commitment. You did not enter your relationship unsure of what you wanted. You were clear. You were open. You were moving with the intention of building something that would last.

Somewhere along the way, you found yourself at a crossroads. A place you never imagined you would be at, especially at this stage of your life. You are caught between making it work and starting over. Between holding on to what you have invested in and letting go of what has not fully chosen you. That space is uncomfortable, and it often arrives quietly, without warning.

Many women around the world find themselves here. Not because they are indecisive, but because they are loyal. Not because they fear commitment, but because they respect it. If you are reading this book, it is not by accident. It is my hope that these words reach you at the exact moment you need clarity most.

This book is written for the woman who is not confused about love, but confused about direction. For the woman who knows what commitment looks like, yet finds herself in a relationship where progress feels implied but never confirmed. Time continues to pass, conversations circle the same points, and patience slowly begins to feel like self-abandonment.

You may have been told to trust the process, to wait a little longer, or to stop putting pressure on the relationship. And while you were willing to give time, you were not willing to give your future to uncertainty. Wanting marriage does not make you demanding. Wanting direction does not make you impatient.

The purpose of this book is not to blame you, and it is not to vilify men. It is to explain how intention works, how affection differs from readiness, and why many relationships remain stuck even when the connection feels real. Some men enter relationships without deciding where they are going. Others know what they want, but not with whom. And a few are already positioned for marriage and move accordingly.

You will not find tactics here on how to convince a man to choose you. What you will find is understanding. You will learn how men think about commitment, why some relationships linger without moving forward, and how to recognize when potential is being mistaken for progress. You will also learn why hope can feel so convincing, even when action never follows.

This book is for the woman who is ready to make an honest decision. Not out of fear, frustration, or pressure, but out of clarity. Because when you understand what you are standing in, you are finally able to decide whether to stay or walk away with peace.

A NOTE ON HOW THIS BOOK UNFOLDS

This book is designed to build gradually. The early chapters may feel reflective or familiar, and that is by design. Many women already sense these patterns emotionally. What often takes time is learning how to recognize them clearly and confidently.

Rather than rushing into conclusions or quick answers, the beginning of the book slows the conversation down so awareness can settle in. That foundation allows the later chapters to move with much more clarity, direction, and practical insight.

If some themes repeat early on, it is because understanding deepens through perspective, not speed. As you continue reading, the ideas will expand and become easier to apply.

WHY HE HASN'T MARRIED *YOU*

1

Dating With Intention vs. Dating for Comfort

HOW MANY WOMEN END UP WITH THE RIGHT MAN AT THE WRONG TIME

Many women do not fall for the wrong man. They fall for a man who feels right, but is not ready to move forward when it actually matters.

You meet someone who checks many of the boxes. He is attractive. He communicates well. He shows emotional presence. He feels stable, familiar, and safe. He looks like the type of man who could become a husband, so it feels natural to assume the timing must also be right.

But timing in relationships has very little to do with age, income, or chemistry. Timing is about decision.

A man can have all the qualities you admire and still be unable to build a future with you because he has not decided what he is willing to commit to. That is where many women get stuck. They are not dealing with bad men. They are dealing with men who have not chosen a direction.

Many men are not wrong in character. They are wrong in capacity.

Meaning, a man may have integrity, kindness, emotional awareness, and strong values, but still lack the internal readiness to fully offer his life to one woman. *Potential* without *access* does not build a future. Availability does.

Think about it practically. Having access to a smaller, real resource is more useful than having no access to a larger one you cannot touch. The same principle applies in relationships. A man who is emotionally appealing but unavailable for commitment cannot build anything meaningful with you, no matter how promising he looks on paper.

This is how women end up with the right man at the wrong time. Not because he lacks character, but because he lacks decision.

THE THREE TYPES OF MEN WHO ENTER RELATIONSHIPS

Most men who enter relationships fall into one of three categories: the Curious Man, the Self-Serving Man, and the Decided Man.

Two of these men often sound alike. The Curious Man and the Self-Serving Man may use similar language. They talk about taking things slow, letting things unfold, and not wanting pressure. Their tone can feel reasonable, calm, and mature.

The Decided Man does not sound like this.

He speaks with clarity. His presence has direction. His intentions show up early, not because he is rushing, but because he already knows what he wants. There is very little ambiguity around why he is there.

Understanding these distinctions can save a woman years of emotional investment.

The Curious Man: Comfort Without Direction

The Curious Man enters a relationship without a clear destination. He is not opposed to marriage, but he has not decided what he wants his future to look like yet. He enjoys connection, companionship, and emotional closeness, but he assumes clarity will arrive later.

He believes time will eventually tell him what to do. Until then, he remains exactly where he is.

The Curious Man often has many qualities that would make him a good partner. He can be consistent, caring, and emotionally available. What he lacks is not character, but direction. He is not avoiding commitment on purpose. He simply has not chosen it.

The Self-Serving Man: Access Without Intention

The Self-Serving Man is not undecided. He already knows the relationship is not leading toward a future. Despite this, he stays.

He avoids clear labels, slows progression, and keeps expectations vague so that he can continue benefiting from the relationship without being required to move it forward. He offers just enough reassurance to keep emotional attachment intact, while never allowing real direction to form.

Hope keeps access alive, so he maintains hope.

Although the Curious Man and the Self-Serving Man can sound similar, their motivations are very different. The Curious Man is uncertain because he has not yet decided what he wants. The Self-Serving Man avoids clarity because clarity would require him to give something up.

One does not know what he wants. The other knows exactly what he does not want and stays anyway.

The Decided Man: Clarity With Purpose

The Decided Man enters a relationship already knowing that marriage is his goal. He is not experimenting with life or dating to pass time. He is confirming alignment while actively demonstrating that he is capable of building a future.

He does not hide behind timing or speak vaguely about direction. His words and actions match. The tone of the relationship feels different early because intention shapes behavior.

Some men believe that choosing a woman internally is enough. They forget that a woman also needs consistency, leadership, emotional safety, and demonstrated stability to trust that he is husband material. The Decided Man understands this. He does not just declare intention. He proves it.

THE QUESTION THAT REVEALS WHICH MAN HE IS

There is a simple way to understand which type of man you are dealing with without pressure or confrontation.

You can ask him, calmly and directly, *"What are you currently dating for right now?"*

This question centers the present rather than the future. It does not ask for promises or timelines. It simply asks him to name his intention.

A Curious Man will usually answer openly but without definition. He may say he is seeing where things go, enjoying the relationship, or open to marriage someday. His uncertainty is genuine.

A Self-Serving Man often avoids the question altogether. He may push back on labels, minimize the importance of direction, or redirect the conversation toward feelings instead of intention. Avoidance protects his access.

A Decided Man answers clearly. He will say that he is dating with marriage in mind. There is no defensiveness and no ambiguity.

If your man seems confused by the question, a simple follow-up removes uncertainty. You can ask, *"Are you dating simply to enjoy a relationship, or are you dating with marriage in mind?"*

His response and reaction will tell you what you need to know. Words alone are not enough.

Patterns reveal truth. A Curious Man gradually moves toward clarity. A Self-Serving Man remains conveniently vague while the relationship stays exactly the same.

These questions reveal where a man currently stands, not who he could become.

WHY WOMEN FALL IN LOVE WITH THE "FUTURE"

There is a psychological reason this pattern repeats so often, and it has very little to do with ignorance, desperation, or poor judgment. It has everything to do with how the human mind behaves once it believes it is moving toward something meaningful.

The brain is wired to support goals that feel purposeful. When you believe your effort is leading somewhere valuable, your mind begins organizing information in ways that reinforce that belief. This happens in careers, personal goals, and especially in relationships. Once the brain accepts a direction, it naturally looks for confirmation that the direction makes sense.

In relationships, this process becomes emotional very quickly.

When you enter a relationship believing it is moving toward marriage or long-term partnership, your mind begins assigning greater meaning to moments of connection, effort, affection, and shared experience. Conversations feel deeper. Small gestures feel symbolic. Time together begins to feel like accumulation rather than simply time passing. These moments start to register internally as progress, even when no external structure has actually changed.

At the same time, information that challenges the imagined future becomes easier to soften or reinterpret. Delays feel temporary instead of significant. Avoidance can get translated into stress or timing issues rather than intentional behavior. Inconsistencies feel situational rather than patterned. **This is not denial. It is the mind protecting emotional investment.**

Your subconscious is not evaluating whether the relationship is objectively aligned. It is focused on preserving emotional continuity. Ending something you have poured energy and time into feels like loss, even when the relationship no longer feels fully secure. So the nervous system leans toward patience and optimism, because those responses reduce emotional disruption. This is not weakness; it is attachment biology doing its job.

The problem emerges when two people are experiencing the same relationship in fundamentally different ways. You may be mentally oriented toward a future you are building toward, while he is emotionally anchored in the present he is enjoying. Your mind is projecting forward. His experience remains rooted in what already feels good. This creates a quiet mismatch in how you are both interpreting the relationship.

You experience time as movement toward something meaningful. He experiences time as confirmation that the current relationship setup is working. Because your attention is directed toward what this relationship *could* become, it becomes harder to fully judge what it actually is *right now*.

When clarity eventually arrives, it often feels emotionally disruptive because it challenges the future your mind has been protecting. It forces a recalibration between imagination and reality. That adjustment can feel painful even when it is healthy and necessary.

This is why dating without intention produces so much internal confusion. Not because the relationship lacks emotional value, but because direction was never clearly defined. Without direction, attachment deepens while alignment remains uncertain. The heart continues moving forward while the structure remains unresolved.

Understanding this pattern helps you tell the difference between feeling close and actually moving forward. Just because the relationship feels deep, familiar, or emotionally strong does not mean it is going anywhere. You can feel connected to someone and still not be building a future together. Spending a lot of time with a man does not mean he intends to move the relationship toward marriage. Time alone does not create direction or commitment. If there is no clear intention being shown through his actions, the future you are holding onto in your mind may never happen in real life.

That is not a failure of effort or love. It is the natural outcome of investing emotionally without established direction.
Confirmation Bias.

WHY DECISION CHANGES EVERYTHING

The core issue in stalled relationships is rarely compatibility. It is *decision.*

A Curious Man may care deeply, but without direction his care does not produce movement. A Self-Serving Man avoids decision because staying vague benefits him. Only a Decided Man moves with intention.

Decision creates clarity. Clarity produces action.

When intention is real, it does not require years to appear. It shows up early through consistency, follow-through, and direction. Love without direction can feel meaningful, but direction is what turns connection into a life. Without it, time becomes something you give instead of something you build.

2

Why Waiting Feels Like Progress

WAITING CAN FEEL LIKE YOU ARE DOING THE RIGHT THING.

Waiting often feels like the mature thing to do. It feels patient, loving, and fair. Staying, giving someone time, and choosing understanding instead of walking away can feel like proof that you are committed, not selfish or cold. For women who truly want to build something real, waiting does not feel lazy. It feels like you are doing the right thing.

Most women are not trying to waste their time. They are trying to build a future with someone they care about. So when a relationship does not move forward right away, giving space can feel wise instead of risky. Waiting can feel like you are being supportive and allowing things to grow naturally instead of forcing something too soon. After a while, waiting starts to feel like work.

You are lowering your expectations, managing your disappointment, staying emotionally open, and sitting with uncertainty about where things are going. That takes energy. Because you are putting in emotional effort, it can feel like progress is happening, even when the relationship itself is not actually changing in any real way.

But putting in emotional effort is not the same thing as the relationship moving forward.

A relationship can take a lot out of you emotionally and still stay stuck in the same place. You can have the same conversations over and over. You can hear the same explanations again and again. Time can keep passing without anything new being built. From the inside, it feels like you are actively working on the relationship. From the outside, nothing is actually moving.

Hope makes this even harder to see.

When you care about someone, hope makes you believe that your patience will eventually pay off. It makes waiting feel meaningful instead of risky. But hope does not change direction on its own. It just makes standing still feel easier to tolerate.

Once you believe a relationship is headed somewhere meaningful, your mind begins treating waiting as part of the process instead of a pause. Time feels like investment rather than delay. Each month feels closer rather than longer, even if no new decisions have been made. This creates an internal sense of momentum that does not always match reality.

Stability adds another layer of confusion. Regular communication, shared routines, emotional familiarity, and physical presence create a sense of security. Stability simply means something is steady, not that it is moving forward. Comfort can exist without direction.

This is where many women become unintentionally anchored.

Waiting feels productive because it demands emotional contribution. But progress is not measured by how much you give. It is measured by whether the relationship is becoming more defined, more intentional, and more future-oriented over time. If months pass and the structure remains unchanged, time is filling the space where a clear decision should be.

HOW MEN EXPERIENCE TIME IN RELATIONSHIPS

Time does not register the same way emotionally for men when the relationship already meets their current needs.

When a man is getting regular attention, emotional closeness, companionship, and stability from a relationship, nothing inside him is telling him that anything needs to change. The relationship works for him in his day-to-day life. Because his needs are being met and nothing feels uncomfortable, there is no internal push for him to move the relationship forward. Without any real loss, tension, or disruption, time does not create urgency. It simply makes the current situation feel more normal and acceptable.

Over time, the relationship starts to feel like part of his everyday life instead of something he needs to seriously think about or decide on.

Talking on the phone regularly becomes routine. Emotional closeness feels normal instead of special. Being together feels expected instead of chosen. Because nothing feels like it is at risk of being taken away, the pressure to make a real decision about the future gets weaker, not stronger.

Comfort slows decision-making.

Decision often comes from tension, contrast, or consequence. When those are absent, there is little psychological motivation to redefine anything. Stability creates a sense of "good enough," which quietly delays intentional movement.

Time then shifts roles. Instead of creating pressure, time becomes permission. Each month that passes without consequence teaches the nervous system that staying undecided carries no cost. The relationship continues smoothly, so there is no internal trigger demanding change.

What feels like waiting to you often feels like equilibrium to him.

You may experience time as emotional risk or uncertainty. He experiences it as consistency and predictability. Without loss, discomfort, or consequence, time does not feel scarce. It feels neutral.

This is not always calculated. Many men are not consciously choosing to delay. They are responding to how the present feels. If the present feels stable, the future does not demand attention.

Patience alone rarely produces movement. Time does not create decision when comfort is high. It deepens the existing pattern.

WHY URGENCY CANNOT BE CREATED, ONLY REVEALED

When a relationship does not naturally move forward, many women begin wondering whether urgency needs to be introduced. The instinct is understandable. If comfort keeps him still, it can feel logical to believe that removing comfort might motivate action. The problem is that urgency and clarity are often confused, even though they operate very differently inside a relationship.

Urgency works by creating pressure. It uses fear, discomfort, or the threat of loss to try to force movement. The goal is to push someone to act, even if they were not already planning to. Clarity is different. Clarity does not try to push a man forward at all. It simply asks him to be honest about what he is doing in the relationship and why he is doing it. When a man only changes his behavior because he feels pressured, he is not making a real choice. He is reacting to discomfort. That reaction can look like progress for a moment, but it is not coming from a genuine internal decision. Once the pressure goes away, he usually goes back to how he was before, because nothing inside him has actually changed.

This is why trying to create urgency rarely leads to real, lasting change. A man may say the right things, talk about the future, or make small adjustments just to calm the situation and restore peace in the relationship. Once things feel comfortable again, the motivation to change disappears, and the original lack of direction is still there. What actually causes a relationship to move forward is not pressure. It is intention. A man who already knows he wants marriage does not need to be pushed into movement. His actions naturally follow the direction he has already decided on. If that inner decision does not exist, no outside tactic, strategy, or pressure will create it.

This is why clarity matters so much. Clarity does not force commitment and it does not set ultimatums. It simply asks a man to be honest about what he is currently building toward in the relationship. Many women avoid asking for clarity, not because the question is unfair, but because the answer might hurt. Not knowing for sure can feel safer than hearing that you two are not moving toward the same future. But staying emotionally attached without clear direction has its own cost. The longer things stay unclear, the more emotional energy gets invested into something that may never move forward.

Clarity is meant to come early, before emotional attachment gets too deep. As a relationship becomes more consistent and emotionally close, it becomes reasonable to understand what direction the other person is moving in. This does not have to be a confrontation or a threat. It is simply a grounded, honest conversation about the present, not about distant hopes or imagined futures.

Choosing not to participate deeper in a relationship that has no direction does not mean punishing him, pulling away emotionally to manipulate him, or trying to scare him into change. It means you stop giving more emotional access, time, and energy to something that has not shown you where it is going. If a man says he is unsure or does not know what he wants, that is taken as the truth right now, not as something you are meant to fix or wait out. Continuing to give more while hoping clarity will appear keeps you emotionally exposed. Protecting your emotional energy until direction is shown is not harsh. It is healthy.

Asking a man what he is dating for right now keeps the conversation grounded in reality instead of fantasy or potential. How he answers, and how comfortable he is answering, tells you much more than promises about the future. A man who is genuinely still figuring things out will usually be open to the question, even if he does not have perfect clarity yet. A self-serving man often avoids giving real answers because clarity would limit his access to you. A man who already knows what he wants answers clearly because his direction is already settled.

Words by themselves are not always enough to tell which one you are dealing with. Patterns over time show intention more clearly than anything a man says in one conversation. A man who is truly reflecting will slowly move toward clearer direction. A man who is protecting his comfort will stay vague because being clear would require him to take responsibility.

Relationships do not stall because women fail to pressure men into moving forward. They stall because the man has not chosen a direction. You cannot make that choice for someone else. You can only observe whether that choice exists by watching consistent behavior and listening to honest communication.

At the end of the day, the only part of this process you truly control is who you are and how you show up. You cannot make a man become ready. You cannot think, love, or wait him into clarity. What you can do is be consistent in your own character. You can show up as the kind of woman you actually are, not a version of yourself shaped by fear of losing him. You can be honest. You can be faithful. You can communicate clearly. You can live in a way that reflects your values. That is your contribution. What he does with that information is his responsibility, not yours.

If you decide that the relationship feels meaningful enough to continue while he figures himself out, that is your choice to make. Waiting is not automatically wrong. The key is that waiting should be intentional on your side, not just emotional. That means you decide, for yourself, how long you are willing to stay in a relationship that has not yet shown clear direction. You set that time frame privately, in your own mind, based on what you need and what you are willing to give.

You do not need to announce your timeline to him. Turning your internal boundary into a deadline often shifts the dynamic from honesty to pressure. It can push him into saying or doing things to meet the time limit rather than because he has genuinely decided. Your time frame is not meant to rush him. It is meant to protect you.

Once you reach the point where you have shown up fully, stayed true to who you are, and given the relationship a fair chance to show direction, the decision becomes yours. If he is still unsure or unwilling to move forward, you are no longer choosing between patience and impatience. You are choosing between remaining in uncertainty or honoring your own needs. That choice is not about punishing him. It is about respecting yourself and your future.

3

Man’s Fear of Marriage

HIS FEAR DISGUISED AS LOGIC

When a man hesitates around marriage, the reason is rarely as simple as timing or circumstances. More often, it is fear. Not fear in a dramatic or obvious sense, but a quiet internal resistance that shows up as hesitation and unresolved uncertainty. This kind of fear does not look panicked. On the surface, it often sounds calm, reasonable, and well thought out.

Many men openly talk about being afraid of marriage. They reference divorce statistics, court systems, and stories they have heard from other men. Online conversations often frame marriage as something risky or unfair to men, creating a shared narrative that normalizes hesitation without ever asking whether the *fear* actually applies to **their real lives**.

Some men have personal reasons for this fear. They may have watched a parent go through a painful divorce or seen a friend lose financial stability, access to his children, or loss of emotional peace. Those experiences leave marks. But many men are not operating from firsthand experience. They are operating from borrowed fear. They inherit anxiety from other people's outcomes without honestly examining whether those outcomes match their own reality.

There is an uncomfortable truth that often gets overlooked. Many men who say they are afraid of losing everything in a divorce do not actually have anything substantial to lose. They are not protecting businesses, estates, or major investments. They are living average lives with average responsibilities. Yet the fear still exists because the fear is not really about money.

Marriage represents permanence. It represents choosing one woman and closing off other options. It introduces responsibility, expectation, and accountability. For men who are uncomfortable with limits, structure, or long-term obligation, that feels threatening regardless of finances. The real fear is not loss of assets. It is loss of flexibility.

Some men also enjoy the benefits of a relationship without wanting the responsibility that commitment brings. They enjoy companionship, intimacy, emotional support, and consistency. Marriage changes that dynamic by introducing shared responsibility and future planning. That shift forces a man to move from enjoying a relationship to building one, and not every man is ready for that transition.

If a man has not addressed this internal resistance, no amount of connection or patience will turn hesitation into clarity. A woman cannot love a man into readiness. Fear has to be confronted internally before progress becomes possible.

Many men frame their hesitation as logic. They talk about being cautious, wanting the timing to feel right, or needing more certainty. But underneath that language is often a deeper discomfort with choosing a direction and staying accountable to it. Commitment forces a man to decide who he is, what he values, and what he is willing to give up in order to build something lasting.

When a man avoids that decision, fear quietly reshapes itself into delay.

If more men focused on their woman and the love they share, fear would not be the issue. Fear becomes an issue when a man is focused on <u>marriage</u> in general instead of the <u>woman</u> he claims to love. To correct this, he would have to stop absorbing everyone else's marriage stories and start creating his own. A man who leads *understands* this. A follower does not.

FEAR OF THE WEDDING AND FEAR OF FINANCIAL LOSS

Sometimes a man is not afraid of being married. He is afraid of the wedding itself. The ceremony can feel overwhelming to him. Standing in front of a crowd. Being the center of attention. Speaking publicly. Having all eyes on him during a moment that feels permanent. For men who are private, reserved, or uncomfortable with attention, the wedding can feel like pressure instead of romance. What looks like hesitation about marriage may actually be discomfort with being publicly put on display.

The planning process can add to that stress. Fittings. Rehearsals. Family expectations. Timelines. The pressure to make the day feel perfect. For some men, the wedding feels like a performance they are expected to deliver rather than a moment they get to experience. The commitment may already feel real to him internally, but the production of the ceremony feels overwhelming. This can cause a man to delay proposing even when he cares deeply, because what he is avoiding is the event, not the life with you.

Another fear that often hides inside marriage hesitation is money. Many men do not fear the marriage license itself. They fear the cost of the wedding. The idea of spending a large amount of money on a single day can feel irresponsible to him, especially if he already feels financial pressure in other areas of his life. If he is struggling with bills, saving, debt, or career stability, a wedding can feel like bad timing rather than a joyful step forward.

Some men view expensive weddings as wasteful when they feel that money could be used for things that feel more practical to them. Paying down debt. Improving living conditions. Buying reliable transportation. Investing in something that lasts longer than one day. In his mind, he may not be rejecting marriage. He may be resisting what he sees as an unnecessary financial burden attached to it.

This becomes confusing for women because the fear gets framed as "not ready for marriage" when the real concern is about the ceremony and the cost surrounding it. A man may think, *"Why spend all that money if we already love each other."* That does not mean marriage has no value to him. It often means the wedding does not feel like a smart or comfortable use of resources in his current situation.

There is also a deeper financial fear tied to divorce. Even men who do not have much right now may worry about what they could lose in the future. They hear stories. They see movies.

They listen to other men talk about losing money, access to their children, or stability in court. The legal side of marriage can feel less like romance and more like a contract with consequences. For some men, marriage begins to feel like inviting the legal system into their personal life, and that thought alone creates resistance.

This fear is often exaggerated, but it still influences behavior. A man may delay commitment because marriage feels like a risk he does not feel prepared to manage. If he has goals, dreams, or future plans, he may worry about what could happen if things did not work out later. Even if that fear is not logical, it still shapes how safe marriage feels to him emotionally.

For men who own businesses, plan to build businesses, or think long-term about financial growth, this fear can feel even heavier. The idea of legal entanglement, possible financial loss, or future disputes can make marriage feel complicated. Even when prenups exist as an option, some men avoid the conversation because bringing it up feels uncomfortable or emotionally loaded.

None of this means marriage is wrong. It means fear often attaches itself to the wedding process, the financial pressure, and the legal consequences, not necessarily to love or partnership itself. A man can want a life with you while still feeling overwhelmed by the structure that marriage introduces around money, law, and public commitment.

This is why clarity matters. If a man is hesitant, it is important to understand what he is actually afraid of. Is he afraid of commitment, or is he afraid of the ceremony. Is he afraid of building a life, or is he afraid of the financial and legal weight attached to how marriage is presented to him. Those are very different fears, and they require very different conversations.

Fear of the wedding can be solved with flexibility. Fear of finances can be solved with planning and honesty. Fear of legal consequences can be addressed with open discussion and boundaries. Fear of commitment cannot be solved externally. That one requires internal decision.

FEAR OF MAKING A PUBLIC PROMISE

Marriage is not only a private decision. It is a public promise. A man is not just committing to you. He is committing in front of family, friends, and witnesses. That public promise carries weight. People expect him to live up to it. People remember it. People hold him accountable to it.

Some men are comfortable with commitment in private but uncomfortable with committing in front of others. The idea that hundreds of people are watching him promise forever can feel heavy. The fear is not about loving you. It is about the pressure of being seen as a man who made a permanent vow.

This is why some men say things like, *"Why do we need to do all that?"* or *"Why do we need to make it such a big deal?"* On the surface, it sounds logical. Underneath, it can be fear of the weight of a public promise. Private love feels manageable. Public commitment feels permanent.

FEAR OF THE DOOR CLOSING FOREVER

For many men, marriage represents the end of searching. It represents closing off all other options. Even when a man loves his partner, the finality of choosing one person for life can trigger discomfort. It is not always about wanting someone else. Sometimes it is about struggling with the idea that the door is permanently closed.

Some men are not walking around thinking, *"She is the only one for me."* They are thinking, *"This is the best choice I have right now."* That difference matters. Curiosity can quietly create hesitation. The thought of *"Is this really it?"* can sit in the background, even when the relationship feels good.

This does not mean he does not care. It means he has not emotionally accepted finality yet. The fear is not of you. It is of closing a chapter of life where options still felt open. Until a man makes peace with finality, commitment will feel heavier than connection.

FEAR SHAPED BY OTHER PEOPLE'S STORIES

Many men are afraid of marriage because of stories they have heard, not experiences they have lived. They absorb narratives from other men, from online spaces, and from divorce horror stories. They hear about men losing money, losing access to their children, or losing peace. Over time, those stories become their expectation of marriage.

This fear is borrowed. It is not built from their own relationship. It is built from other people's outcomes. Some men do not stop to ask whether those situations actually match their own lives. They inherit anxiety without checking whether the same risks apply to them personally.

This is why a man can be in a healthy relationship and still talk as if marriage is dangerous. He is reacting to a story, not to the reality in front of him. Until he separates his relationship from other people's outcomes, fear can shape his decisions more than the woman he is actually with.

WHEN FEAR TURNS INTO DELAY

Fear rarely announces itself directly. It usually shows up as postponement. A man who is afraid of commitment does not say he is afraid. He simply keeps everything comfortable while avoiding forward movement. This is where many women become confused.

On the surface, the relationship looks stable. He communicates, shows affection, and enjoys your presence. Nothing appears broken. But beneath that stability is a refusal to define the future. By delaying decisions, he avoids responsibility while continuing to benefit from the relationship. Time becomes a buffer between him and accountability.

Delay often gets mistaken for caution. Women are taught that patience reflects maturity and that moving slowly shows wisdom. But there is a difference between a man who is preparing and a man who is stalling. Preparation has direction. Stalling maintains comfort.

A man who is preparing may move gradually, but his actions still point forward. Conversations become clearer. Future plans become more specific. Responsibility increases over time. A man who is stalling keeps the relationship emotionally warm but structurally unchanged. Months pass, routines deepen, but nothing evolves.

When fear drives delay, timelines stay vague. He may say he needs more time but cannot explain what needs to change for readiness to arrive. Important conversations soften or drift into reassurance rather than resolution. Delay without clarity is not patience. It is avoidance.

Fear-driven delay allows a man to stay in control without openly rejecting the future. He does not have to say no. He simply keeps saying not yet. Over time, not yet produces the same result as no, just more quietly.

What matters is not how long he has stayed. What matters is what has changed because he stayed.

Some men genuinely grow over time. Growth creates visible movement. Fear-driven delay creates repetition. When a relationship feels emotionally full but directionally empty, fear is often operating underneath the surface.

At some point, delay stops being neutral. It becomes a decision of its own. When that happens, waiting no longer serves love. It only protects comfort.

You do not measure progress by how often he calls, how long you have been together, or how peaceful the relationship feels. You measure progress by whether the relationship is becoming more defined, more intentional, and more future-oriented over time. If months pass and the structure remains exactly the same, time is filling the space where a clear decision should be.

Real structure shows up in how two people begin organizing their lives together instead of simply enjoying each other's presence. It looks like conversations that move beyond feelings and into responsibility. It means talking openly about money, spending habits, debt, savings, and long-term financial goals, not as curiosity, but as preparation. It means learning how each other handles pressure, conflict, and accountability, because those patterns matter far more in marriage than chemistry ever will. Structure shows up when decisions begin to affect both people instead of remaining separate and individual. You start seeing alignment in how time is prioritized, how future plans are made, and how lifestyle choices are shaped with each other in mind.

Structure also shows up spiritually and emotionally. For couples grounded in faith, that can mean praying together, reading scripture together, or having real conversations about values, boundaries, and how each person lives out their beliefs. It means seeing whether your morals, discipline, and worldview actually align when life gets routine, not just when emotions are high. Spiritually aligned couples do not only talk about God in theory. They practice faith in the way they treat each other, solve problems, manage stress, and make decisions. Those habits reveal whether two people are building something rooted or simply sharing moments.

Practical structure matters just as much. It shows up in discussions about where you would live, how you would raise children, how you handle family boundaries, how you divide responsibility, and what kind of life you are actually trying to build together. These conversations do not stay hypothetical forever in a progressing relationship. They begin turning into plans, timelines, and real-world adjustments. When a man is serious about building, his language slowly shifts from comfort to construction, from enjoying what is to shaping what will be.

When none of this is happening, the relationship may feel loving and stable, but it is not being built into anything. Time passes, memories deepen, attachment grows, yet nothing becomes clearer, firmer, or more intentional. That is not structure. That is familiarity. And familiarity can keep two people emotionally connected for years without ever moving them toward a shared future.

You avoid delay by watching patterns, not promises. You avoid delay by noticing whether clarity is increasing or disappearing. You avoid delay by understanding that consistency without direction does not protect your future.

Most importantly, you avoid delay by refusing to substitute patience for purpose. Time does not create readiness. Decision does. And when decision is absent, waiting does not move you closer to marriage. It only keeps you standing in the same place longer.

That awareness is what protects you.

HIS PEACE AND SPACE

Many men spend their lives trying to build something solid. They want stability. They want security. They want to reach a place where they feel capable of supporting a family one day, even if they are not ready for that step yet. A highly functioning man often takes pride in creating a life that works. He works hard. He builds routines. He creates a sense of order around himself. Over time, he becomes used to moving through life alone while he is building. That quiet becomes normal to him. Eventually, that quiet becomes comfortable.

After a while, some men become attached to that comfort. They start to see their solitude as peace. They get used to making decisions without having to consider anyone else. They get used to controlling their schedule, their space, their money, and their time. So when a woman enters his life, even a woman he cares about, it can feel like a threat to the rhythm he has built. Not because he does not like her, but because her presence changes the environment he has learned to feel safe in.

These men often still allow short term relationships, casual dating, or physical connections. Those feel manageable because they do not require him to reshape his daily life. A long-term relationship feels different. It feels like disruption. He may not describe it as fear. He often describes it as choosing peace. In his mind, protecting his peace means protecting his routines, his space, and his independence from being altered by someone else's needs.

You can see this show up in small, everyday ways. He likes his place the way it is. His room is set up how he wants it. His schedule runs how he likes it. His habits feel efficient to him. The idea of someone coming into his space, rearranging things, leaving things around, wanting shared routines, or changing how he lives can feel intrusive to him. It is not really about furniture or space. It is about control.

For these men, it is not that they are against women. It is not that they are against commitment in theory. It is the day-to-day reality of shared life that feels heavy to them. It is the loss of total freedom over their environment. It is the adjustment of no longer moving through life completely unchecked. The quiet they built alone feels fragile to them, and they are afraid of losing it.

People often say your partner should be your peace. But for these men, peace was created before the relationship ever existed. Their peace came from solitude, routine, and emotional distance. So when a relationship begins to ask for shared space, shared decisions, and shared emotional presence, it does not feel like peace to them. It feels like disruption of a system that already works for them.

Underneath all of this, the deeper issue is usually fear of choosing the wrong partner. He is not afraid of partnership itself. He is afraid of choosing someone who will disturb his life instead of fitting into it. He is afraid that letting someone close will bring chaos into a structure he worked hard to build. If he were confident in his ability to choose a healthy partner, he would not feel the same level of resistance. But past experiences, poor choices, or emotional wounds often make him cautious.

So instead of saying, *"I am afraid I might choose wrong,"* he says, *"I am protecting my peace."* Instead of admitting uncertainty, he creates distance. Not because the woman is wrong for him, but because he is unsure of his own judgment. And when that uncertainty exists, keeping emotional space feels safer than risking disruption of the life he has learned to control.

THE FREEDOM OF MANY WOMEN

Earlier, we talked about a man's fear of permanence when it comes to marriage. But the fear is not just about the wedding itself. For many men, the deeper fear is the idea of choosing one woman for life. It is the fear of closing the door on all other possibilities. Not because those possibilities were real in the first place, but because the idea of having options feels powerful to him.

This fear is strange because, in many cases, it is about losing access to women he never truly had. He scrolls through social media and sees women he will never meet, never date, and never have a real chance with. But in his mind, marriage feels like it removes those women from the table. The illusion of endless options feels like freedom. Commitment feels like limitation. So he experiences marriage as loss, even when nothing tangible is actually being taken from him.

Some men, however, do have real-life access to other women. Old situations. Exes who still answer the phone. Women he exchanged numbers with but never fully closed the door on. Flirtations that stay just close enough to feel like backup options. These are the connections he fears losing when the idea of permanence comes up. To him, marriage feels like giving up access, attention, and potential attention from other women, even if those connections are shallow, inconsistent, or unhealthy.

This is why some men enter marriage already planning to cheat. Not because they hate their partner, but because cheating is the only way they can mentally accept the idea of permanence. In their mind, marriage is tolerable as long as they believe their access to other women will never fully disappear. They do not marry because they are fully ready to choose one woman. They marry because they believe they can have one woman publicly while still preserving their sense of options privately. The ring does not feel like an ending to their freedom. It feels like a performance piece. That reality, painful as it is, explains why so many women end up married to men who were never truly exclusive in their hearts.

A man who fears losing options often thinks about women the same way he thinks about a meal. His favorite meal may be steak, but the idea of eating steak every day makes him feel restricted. While a woman is not a product, self-serving men often carry this same mindset into relationships. They want the comfort of one stable woman while still wanting access to novelty, attention, and validation from others.

This is not about love. This is about appetite. A man who fears permanence is not wrestling with whether he cares about you. He is wrestling with whether he is willing to let go of the version of himself that wants endless access to options. Until he makes peace with choosing one person over many possibilities, commitment will always feel like loss instead of choice.

4

The Illusion of Progress

WHY COMFORT FEELS LIKE GROWTH

A relationship can feel emotionally deep while staying structurally stuck. You can talk more. Open up more. Spend more time together. Feel closer. Feel more bonded. All of that can be real. But emotional closeness does not automatically change where the relationship is going. A relationship can feel full while still not being built toward anything.

Real progress changes the shape of the relationship. It adds structure. It adds shared responsibility. It changes how decisions are made. It creates movement in real life, not just emotional connection. When a relationship is progressing, the future slowly becomes shared, not just talked about. Plans begin to include both people. Life choices begin to reflect the relationship. The relationship starts to carry weight beyond the present moment.

When a relationship is only continuing, reassurance replaces movement. He says the right things to calm your worries, but nothing in the relationship actually changes. The bond grows, but the structure stays the same. Affection increases, but direction does not. The relationship feels emotionally alive while remaining directionally frozen.

Over time, many women begin to adjust themselves to make this feel easier. They notice which conversations cause tension and which ones keep the peace. They soften expectations. They delay hard questions. They stop asking for clarity in order to protect the relationship from discomfort. This adjustment often feels like emotional maturity. It feels like patience. It feels like understanding. In reality, it is often accommodation.

Compromise means two people adjust in order to move toward the same destination. Accommodation means one person reshapes themselves so the relationship can continue without a destination. When accommodation becomes the main way the relationship stays peaceful, long-term progress becomes unlikely because the relationship no longer requires direction.

This pattern usually appears in more than one area of a man's life. If he stays in jobs he admits are not going anywhere, avoids necessary transitions, or delays difficult decisions elsewhere, he is showing how much comfort guides his choices. This is not about judging character. It is about recognizing patterns. A man who avoids structural change in his life often avoids structural change in relationships too.

Real progress leaves evidence. It shows up in behavior, not just reassurance. It shows up when responsibility is shared. When planning becomes real instead of abstract. When decisions begin to include the future, not just the present. When the relationship starts to shape how life is lived, not just how feelings are felt.

Men do not casually bring long-term responsibility into relationships they do not see as long-term. When a man is serious, the relationship begins to take up space in his planning, his priorities, and his decisions. Not because he is pressured, but because his intention has already shifted.

Marriage does not come from waiting long enough, loving hard enough, or being patient enough. It comes from decision, alignment, and two people building something on purpose. When months pass and nothing about the relationship structure changes, time is not moving the relationship forward. Time is simply allowing the relationship to continue without direction.

HE IS NOT CONFUSED ABOUT YOU

Many women explain a stalled relationship by saying he is confused. He does not know what he wants yet. He needs more time. He is still figuring things out. That explanation feels easier to sit with because it keeps the relationship open and gives hope that things will change. But confusion and comfort are not the same thing, and mixing them up is how women end up waiting far longer than they ever planned to.

A man who is truly confused is still sorting himself out. He may not know what kind of life he wants yet. He may still be trying to figure out his direction, his goals, or whether he even wants a serious relationship right now. His hesitation comes from not having answers yet. Over time, a confused man becomes clearer. His thinking sharpens. His direction becomes more defined.

A comfortable man is different. A comfortable man already knows what his life looks like, and he likes it the way it is. He has companionship. He has routine. He has emotional access. He has consistency. And he gets all of that without having to build a long-term relationship with you. The relationship fits into his life without requiring him to change anything about how he lives. From his point of view, nothing feels broken, so nothing feels urgent.

When a man does not move forward, it is easy to assume he is still figuring things out. In many cases, there is nothing left for him to figure out. He is not confused. He is settled into a situation that works for him. He checks in. He spends time with you. He shows affection. He may even talk loosely about the future. But none of that requires him to choose a long-term relationship with you. It only allows him to keep enjoying what already feels good.

When comfort gets mistaken for confusion, women often respond by being more patient, more understanding, and more flexible. They think that if they give him enough time, support, and space, he will eventually choose them. In reality, the more comfortable his life becomes, the less reason he has to change anything. Over time, he is not moving closer to choosing you. He is becoming more comfortable not choosing at all.

This is why many men delay without ever directly saying no. Most men who do not want a long-term relationship with a woman do not sit her down and say, *"I do not see a future with you."* Saying that would cost him access, comfort, and emotional connection. So instead of closing the door, he leaves it cracked open. He stays present enough to keep the relationship alive, but undefined enough to avoid building anything real.

Delay often sounds reasonable. He may say he wants to make sure the relationship is solid before taking the next step. He may say he believes in letting things happen naturally. He may say he does not want to rush something important. None of those statements are wrong by themselves. The problem is what never follows. There is no real movement toward a long-term relationship with you. There is no shift in how the relationship is built.

Sometimes delay shows up when talking about the future gets framed as pressure. When you bring up where things are going, he may say you are stressing him out or moving too fast. Over time, this trains you to stop asking. You start protecting the relationship from uncomfortable conversations instead of protecting yourself from being in a situation that is not going anywhere.

Another way delay shows up is through reassurance without change. He may say he cares about you. He may say he is happy with you. He may show affection and even do thoughtful things. But caring about you and staying with you is not the same as choosing a long-term relationship with you. Reassurance can calm your anxiety while the relationship stays exactly where it is. Months and years can pass this way without anything actually changing.

The difference between honest uncertainty and intentional delay shows up in what time produces. A man who is genuinely unsure still talks honestly about the future. He does not dodge the conversation. He does not circle the same answers forever. Over time, his thinking becomes clearer and his behavior starts showing direction. A man who is delaying keeps the conversation emotional instead of directional. He focuses on how good things feel instead of where things are going. Time helps him stay comfortable, not move forward.

WHAT HE'S SUPPOSED TO SOUND LIKE

When a man actually knows what he wants with you, you do not feel confused after talking to him. You may not have every detail figured out yet, but you walk away from the conversation knowing where you stand. He does not dodge questions about the future. He does not give answers that sound good but mean nothing. He is able to say, in normal language, whether he is building toward a long-term relationship with you or not.

In real life, this means his words sound grounded and specific, not dreamy and open ended. He does not keep you floating on phrases like, *"Let's just see how things go,"* or *"We'll figure it out someday,"* while expecting you to keep showing up fully. Even if he is still figuring out timing, he is clear about intention. You are not guessing whether you are just something temporary in his life.

This does not mean he is rushing you into marriage or making big promises early. It means he is honest about what direction he is dating in. A man who wants a long-term relationship does not treat the relationship like a casual experience. He dates with a purpose. You do not have to decode his tone, analyze his wording, or read between the lines. You are not left trying to interpret what he meant by vague statements while giving him your time, your body, and your emotional energy.

When a man knows what he wants, he does not get uncomfortable when the future comes up. He does not make you feel like you are asking for too much just for wanting to know where things are going. He understands that being honest about direction protects both people from wasting time. You are not trying to change his mind. You are simply finding out what his mind is already set on.

When that honesty is missing, you start to feel it in your body and your thoughts. You replay conversations. You wonder if you asked the question the wrong way. You feel uneasy even after spending time together. You tell yourself things are good, but something feels off. That heaviness is not you being dramatic. It is your intuition reacting to being emotionally involved in something that is not being built toward anything real.

A man can care about you, enjoy your company, and feel close to you while still not wanting a long-term relationship with you. Those things are not the same. Feeling close does not mean he is choosing a future with you. If months or years pass and nothing about the relationship is becoming more serious in real life ways, then waiting is not helping him figure it out. Waiting is simply allowing him to stay in a situation that works for him while your life stays on hold.

5

The Woman He Married In His Mind

THE MENTAL WIFE

Over time, many men do not fall in love with a real woman. They fall in love with an idea they have quietly been building in their mind for years.

This idea does not come from one relationship or one woman. It is formed from many experiences layered together over time. A man notices qualities he likes in different women and begins collecting them mentally, often without realizing it.

He dates one woman and admires her body. He sees another woman online and likes her hair. He meets someone who goes to church and respects her values. He knows a woman who stays disciplined in her health and respects her consistency. He dates another woman who creates peace at home and enjoys how she nurtures. None of these women are the same person, yet he quietly gathers pieces from each of them.

Over the years, those pieces begin forming a composite woman in his mind. She has never existed in one body, one personality, or one life. She exists only as a mental construction. That is the Mental Wife.

The Mental Wife is perfect because she cannot disappoint him. She never has bad days unless he imagines them. She never changes in ways he does not approve of. She never asks for more than he wants to give. She never challenges him at inconvenient moments. She never requires growth before he feels ready. Because she is imaginary, she remains endlessly convenient.

This is where many women unknowingly compete with something they can never outpace. A real woman will always fall short of a woman who only exists in a man's mind. A real woman has moods, needs, expectations, history, and growth. She evolves with life. The Mental Wife does not. She stays frozen in whatever version feels most comfortable to him in that season.

When a man carries this mental image, he can genuinely care about the woman he is dating and still feel unsatisfied. Not because she lacks value, but because she is real. She cannot embody every trait he has mentally stitched together from years of exposure and imagination.

This is one of the quiet reasons a man can remain in a relationship without moving forward. He enjoys the relationship, yet he continues measuring the woman in front of him against a standard that cannot be fulfilled. Even if he is not consciously aware of it, his hesitation reflects this internal comparison.

Marriage requires choosing one real person fully and releasing imagined alternatives. A man who remains attached to his Mental Wife experiences commitment as loss rather than gain. Choosing one woman feels like surrendering endless possibilities rather than building something meaningful.

This is why some men delay even when the relationship appears strong on paper. The woman may be loving, loyal, supportive, and emotionally present, yet she is still being compared to a moving internal ideal. Every new exposure subtly reshapes that fantasy. The standard shifts, and the finish line keeps moving.

The tragedy of the Mental Wife is that she keeps a man emotionally unsettled while appearing stable. He may remain in the relationship, benefit from intimacy and companionship, and appear consistent, yet never feel fully ready to choose. From the outside it may look like fear or confusion. Internally, it is attachment to an imagined perfection that cannot be satisfied.

This is not about any woman failing to be enough. It is about a man never closing the door on imagined options. As long as the Mental Wife remains active in his mind, no real woman will ever feel final.

BREAKING THE MENTAL WIFE

The idea of the *Mental Wife* stays alive because a man's life setup allows it to stay alive. As long as he can have companionship, emotional support, intimacy, and consistency without having to make a real decision, there is no pressure for him to let go of the fantasy. Nothing in his daily life is forcing him to choose, so the imagined version of "the perfect woman" never has to be challenged.

This is often where women unknowingly help keep the fantasy alive. When a woman stays in a relationship without clarity, the man learns that indecision does not cost him anything. When expectations are lowered to keep the peace, he never has to face the gap between fantasy and reality. When a woman gives him deep emotional access and commitment without requiring direction, the fantasy stays protected. This is usually not done on purpose. It is just how the relationship ends up being structured.

The fantasy is not broken by love. A man can care deeply and still hold on to an imaginary ideal. Emotional connection by itself does not force someone to grow up or make a choice. What actually disrupts fantasy is consequence.

The fantasy starts to lose power when indecision begins to cost him something real. When access is no longer guaranteed, when comfort is disrupted, and when your presence is no longer something he can assume will always be there, the imagined woman loses her safety net. Reality forces him to compare what he imagined with what he is actually about to lose.

This is why many men only realize what they had after they lose it. Comfort allows fantasy to survive. Loss forces reality to show up.

Letting go of the Mental Wife also takes maturity. A man has to understand that marriage is not about finding one woman who has every single trait he has ever liked in different women. Marriage is falling in love with a real woman and all her real-world gifts and faults. Marriage is choosing one real woman fully and accepting that choosing means giving up other nonexistent options. Until he sees choosing one person as growth instead of loss, fantasy will always feel safer than commitment.

Women cannot compete with a fantasy. You cannot outwork it with patience. You cannot out-love it. You cannot earn your way past it by being better. Letting go of the fantasy is work only the man can do for himself. If he has not done that internal work, no amount of devotion will turn him into a husband.

Marriage becomes possible only when fantasy is released. Until then, every real woman may feel close, but never final. That is not a reflection of your value. It reflects a man who has not chosen reality over imagination.

6

The Permanent Boyfriend Setup

THE PERMANENT BOYFRIEND

Before you can understand how the permanent boyfriend setup works, you have to understand the type of man who creates it. This man is not mainly defined by whether he lies or tells the truth. He is defined by how he protects his comfort and limits his risk. His primary goal is not building toward something. It is maintaining access to the benefits of a relationship without increasing responsibility.

A self-serving man does not lie all the time, and he does not tell the truth because he is grounded in strong values. His honesty shifts depending on how secure he feels in his position with you. When he believes you are emotionally invested and unlikely to leave, he feels safe being more honest. At that point, honesty does not threaten his access. He can admit what he does not want, what he is not ready for, or what he has no intention of offering because he assumes the relationship will continue anyway.

When he is not sure how attached you are, the way he talks to you changes. If he feels like you might pull back, walk away, or start asking where things are going before he feels secure in the relationship, he becomes more careful with what he says. In those moments, he is not lying to hurt you. He is protecting what he is getting. He holds back the truth to keep the relationship going. He avoids being direct because being direct might cost him the comfort, routine, or intimacy he enjoys before he is ready to give it up.

This is why honesty often shows up later instead of early on. Once he feels confident that you are emotionally invested and unlikely to leave, telling the truth feels safer to him. At that point, he may suddenly admit that he does not believe in marriage, that he likes things exactly how they are, or that he has no plans to change the relationship. From his point of view, the risk is gone. He assumes you are not going anywhere, so he no longer feels pressure to protect your expectations.

When he is not sure that you are fully locked in yet, he is more likely to talk in ways that keep you around without actually choosing a direction. He may mention the future in a vague way without saying what that future looks like. He may hint at progress without taking real steps toward it. He may stretch timelines and give soft answers instead of clear ones. This is not him being confused. It is him managing comfort. He is trying to keep the relationship exactly how it benefits him, without making decisions that would change what he currently gets from it.

This is why words alone are unreliable with this type of man. His honesty is not guided by principle. It is guided by what protects his position. When honesty feels safe, he speaks freely. When honesty feels risky, he speaks in ways that preserve access. In both cases, the goal is the same. Keep the relationship functioning without increasing obligation.

This behavior creates the foundation of the permanent boyfriend setup. The situation is rarely accidental, and it is not usually a misunderstanding. It is the result of a relationship being built in a way that allows him to receive companionship, emotional support, intimacy, and consistency without ever being required to move toward shared responsibility.

Some men do not delay marriage because they are unsure or emotionally stuck. They delay marriage because the relationship already works for them as it is. Their needs are being met without requiring them to restructure their life, make permanent decisions, or take on shared risk. The relationship becomes a stable arrangement rather than a path toward building a future.

A man who enjoys your presence, your emotional support, your physical access, and your consistency while maintaining separate homes, separate finances, and no defined future is not slowly moving toward marriage. He is maintaining a structure that protects his comfort and limits his risk. The separation is not temporary. It is functional. His life remains intact whether the relationship continues or ends.

This is why these men can sound honest when they talk. They may say they are not ready for marriage. They may say they care about you and do not want to rush. They may even say they enjoy what you have together. What they are not doing is changing the structure of the relationship in a way that requires growth. Their words can sound sincere while their behavior reveals that comfort has already been chosen over building something permanent.

A man who plans to marry does not build his life around avoiding shared responsibility. He does not create a relationship that only works as long as nothing permanent is expected of him. He understands that marriage involves shared decisions, shared risk, and shared direction, and his behavior begins moving in that direction long before a proposal ever happens.

The permanent boyfriend avoids that shift. He may care about you. He may enjoy your company. He may even love you in the way that feels real to him. What he protects most is the version of the relationship that allows him to remain unchanged. He wants closeness without commitment and companionship without accountability. As long as the relationship lets him stay comfortable, he has no internal reason to disrupt it.

When a man remains in a relationship for years, it is easy to mistake his presence for progress. But staying is not the same as building. Staying is easy when leaving would cost comfort, intimacy, and convenience. Staying does not mean he is choosing a future with you. It often means he is choosing the arrangement that benefits him. Arrangements do not naturally evolve into marriages.

A relationship that does not require growth, leadership, or commitment is functioning exactly as it was designed to function. Waiting inside that structure does not move you closer to marriage. It confirms that the limits he has already set are acceptable to you. This is not romance or patience. It is tolerating a setup that protects his comfort while placing your future on pause.

WHY THIS TYPE OF MAN TELLS THE TRUTH SOMETIMES AND LIES AT OTHER TIMES

At some point, many women notice something confusing. There are moments when he suddenly sounds honest. He may admit that he is not ready for marriage, that he does not want anything serious, or that he is unsure about the future. In those moments, the honesty can feel relieving because it feels better than guessing. Even when the truth hurts, it can feel grounding to finally hear something direct. What often goes unnoticed is not the honesty itself, but the conditions under which it appears.

With this type of man, honesty shows up when it does not interfere with the structure of the relationship. He speaks freely when he believes the relationship will continue regardless of what he says, or when he does not care whether it continues at all. In both situations, honesty does not threaten his comfort, access, or position. The truth feels safe because it does not require him to change anything about how the relationship is functioning.

When he believes you are deeply invested and unlikely to walk away, he feels comfortable being blunt. He may admit that he does not want marriage, that he enjoys the relationship as it is, or that he has no plans to move forward. From his perspective, the relationship is already stable. He does not feel pressure to protect the bond because he assumes your attachment will keep it intact. In this phase, honesty costs him nothing because he does not believe it will change the structure of what he is receiving.

The same dynamic appears when he does not care about losing you. If the relationship is low investment for him, he may speak very directly about not wanting commitment or not seeing a future together. In that case, honesty feels easy because there is nothing to protect. If you stay, he benefits. If you leave, he does not feel much loss. The truth comes out freely because the outcome does not matter to him.

The most confusing stage happens in between those two states. This is the stage where he wants to keep the relationship but does not want to commit to it. He enjoys your presence, the comfort you bring, and the stability of the connection, but he does not want to change the structure of his life. In this space, honesty becomes inconvenient. Telling the full truth might lead to consequences he does not want, such as losing access to you, being asked to step up, or having to make a decision.

When he senses that honesty could disrupt the relationship, his language shifts. Answers become vague. Timelines stretch without definition. Conversations circle around the topic of the future without landing anywhere specific. He may reassure you emotionally while avoiding clear direction. He may talk about enjoying what you have, taking things slow, or letting things unfold, without naming what he is actually building toward. The goal is not clarity. The goal is to keep the relationship comfortable and intact.

In this phase, dishonesty is rarely dramatic. It shows up as avoiding certain conversations, delaying answers, softening intentions, or offering half-truths that calm you without requiring him to change. He gives enough reassurance to maintain emotional access, but not enough truth to force a decision. This is not about wanting to hurt you. It is about wanting to keep the benefits of the relationship without taking on more responsibility.

This is where a lot of women misunderstand what is really happening. Because he can be caring, show up, and sometimes tell the truth, it is easy to think the problem is that he is confused about his feelings or unsure about what he wants. In many cases, he is not confused at all. The issue is not his emotions. The issue is how the relationship is set up. He controls how much truth you get based on what helps him keep the relationship comfortable for himself. When telling the truth will not change anything or cost him anything, he tells it. When telling the truth might lead to you pulling back, asking for more, or leaving, he softens it or avoids it. His honesty goes up and down depending on what helps keep the relationship the way he likes it, not because he is trying to become clearer about the future.

This is why his words can change from one moment to the next. One conversation can feel real, open, and grounding, and the next conversation can feel vague, confusing, or like you are going in circles. It can feel like clarity is right there, but somehow you never fully get it. The truth is not missing. It is being given in small pieces that do not force him to change anything about the relationship. He shares just enough to keep things calm, but not enough to move the relationship forward.

A man who is actually ready to commit does not move like this. He does not change how honest he is based on whether you might stay or leave. He does not shape the truth to protect his access to you. He speaks plainly because he already knows what he wants and is willing to accept whatever happens because of that honesty. His words and his actions point in the same direction because the relationship is actually moving toward something real and defined.

The permanent boyfriend is different. He is okay with you staying in the relationship even though he is not choosing you fully. He is comfortable being honest only when it does not cost him anything. When telling the full truth might disturb the comfort of the relationship, he replaces truth with reassurance to keep things smooth. That is not emotional confusion. That is him keeping the relationship in a form that works for him.

Understanding this helps break the belief that more time, more patience, or more love will eventually make him fully honest and clear. He already knows how to be honest. He is choosing when honesty benefits him. Once you see this pattern, the real question is no longer whether he tells the truth sometimes. The real question becomes whether his honesty ever puts him at risk of losing you.

If telling the truth never costs him anything, then the relationship is not stuck because he does not know what he wants. It is stuck because the way the relationship is set up allows him to keep getting what he wants without having to move forward.

HOW TO AVOID THE MAN WHO NEVER PLANS TO CHOOSE YOU

Avoiding this type of man does not require playing games, manipulating situations, or becoming emotionally hardened. It requires having structure in how you move, setting clear personal boundaries, and being willing to accept information early instead of negotiating against it later. Most women do not end up stuck in these relationships because they failed to notice warning signs. They end up stuck because they explained the warning signs away. They told themselves he just needed time, assumed his hesitation meant something other than lack of intention, and believed that patience would eventually turn comfort into commitment.

One of the clearest ways to spot this pattern early is to listen to how a man talks about commitment itself, not just how he talks about you. He may praise your personality, your looks, or the connection you share, while speaking negatively or vaguely about marriage and long-term responsibility. He might describe marriage as stressful, unnecessary, or limiting, even while saying how much he enjoys being with you. **When a man separates how he feels about you from how he feels about marriage, that separation matters.** It shows that enjoyment and commitment live in two different categories for him, and liking you does not automatically mean he wants to build a life with you.

Another important signal is how he reacts when clarity is introduced, not how he behaves when things feel easy. If he becomes defensive, downplays the importance of defining the future, or frames your desire for clarity as pressure, that response is not confusion. It is protection of a structure that allows him to keep enjoying the relationship without having to take on the responsibility of a wife.

You can also learn a lot by noticing where his limits show up. This type of man often has no problem with emotional closeness, physical intimacy, or spending regular time together, but becomes hesitant when responsibility enters the conversation. He may prefer to live separately indefinitely, keep finances completely separate with no plan to ever combine, or avoid labels because they "complicate things." These choices are not neutral preferences. They are design choices. He is shaping a relationship that gives him companionship and consistency without requiring him to step into long-term responsibility.

It is also important to stop treating time as neutral. Time teaches people what is allowed and what will be tolerated. When weeks and months pass without structural change, the relationship is teaching him that delay carries no consequence. If you remain fully available and emotionally invested while the structure of the relationship never evolves, you are confirming that the current setup works for him. Consistency without direction is not stability. It is stagnation that feels comfortable because nothing is being challenged.

Another common trap is slowly lowering your own standards to keep the relationship peaceful. At first, this feels like patience, flexibility, or emotional maturity. Over time, those small adjustments add up. The relationship begins revolving around what keeps him comfortable instead of what moves both of you forward. Avoiding this man requires being honest with yourself about whether your standards are actually being met, or whether you are quietly reshaping your expectations to fit the limits of what he is willing to offer.

It also helps to observe how he handles responsibility in other areas of his life. A man who avoids difficult decisions at work, stays in situations he admits have no future, or repeatedly postpones necessary change often brings that same pattern into relationships. While people can grow, patterns still matter. If he consistently chooses comfort over progress in other areas, it is unlikely he will suddenly choose differently when it comes to long-term commitment with you.

Most importantly, believe what he tells you the first time. When a man says he does not want commitment, does not believe in marriage, or is unsure about building a future, take that information seriously. Do not treat those statements as temporary moods you are meant to manage or outgrow. Waiting for his behavior to contradict what he has already told you often turns into years spent hoping comfort will somehow become intention.

This is not about leaving at the first sign of uncertainty. It is about refusing to build a life with someone who benefits from keeping the relationship undefined. A man who wants marriage moves toward it through his behavior and the structure he creates. A man who wants comfort designs a relationship that allows him to stay comfortable without having to choose.

Two simple actions can help protect you early on. Once consistency is established, ask what he is dating for right now, and then watch what actually changes over the next few months. If the relationship structure remains the same, treat that as real information rather than a temporary phase. In addition, set a personal boundary around access. Decide what level of access you will not offer without direction, whether that involves living together, combining finances, doing wife-level labor, or remaining exclusive without clarity. This boundary is not meant to punish him. It is meant to protect your time, your energy, and your future.

Avoiding this type of man does not mean avoiding love or connection. It means choosing relationships where effort is matched with direction, where care is paired with responsibility, and where your time is treated as valuable rather than convenient. The goal is not to convince a man to become ready. The goal is to recognize readiness before emotional attachment makes reality harder to accept.

7

How Long Is Too Long to Wait for a Man to Marry You?

WHEN A MAN IS ACTUALLY INTENTIONAL

When a man starts dating and already knows he wants marriage one day, he moves differently from the beginning. He is not just dating to kill time or see where things go years from now. He is paying attention on purpose. He is asking himself, *"Can I actually build a life with this woman?"* He is not looking for a perfect woman. He is looking to see if the basics are there for a real future together.

Because of that, it usually does not take him years to decide. He is not waiting for time to magically convince him. He is watching how you live day to day, how you think, and how you move through life. He knows that how someone lives matters more long-term than just having chemistry or good vibes.

He notices how you handle money. Not because he wants to control you, but because money becomes shared in real relationships. He pays attention to whether you are reckless with spending or thoughtful, whether you live within your means, and whether you are honest about how you handle finances. He is not looking for you to be rich. He is looking to see if you are responsible and consistent, because that affects a household.

If you have kids, he watches how you treat them. He notices your patience, how you discipline, and how you talk about being a mother. If you do not have kids, he listens to how you talk about having them in the future. He wants to know if you have really thought about it and whether your values line up with the kind of family life he wants. These are real life questions to him, not just casual talk.

He also pays attention to how you think about your future. Where do you want to live. Do you think about building stability, or do you mostly live for what feels good right now. He does not need you to have the same exact dreams as him, but he needs to see that your direction in life is compatible with his.

He notices how you deal with stress, conflict, and accountability. When you talk about your job, your friends, or problems in your life, does everyone else always seem to be the problem. Or can you take responsibility for your part. Do you carry a lot of bitterness, or are you generally grounded. These patterns matter because marriage brings daily stress, and how you normally handle life becomes how the relationship feels long-term.

He also pays attention to your relationship with your mother. Not because it has to be perfect, but because it often shows how you handle closeness, boundaries, and emotional repair. Does your relationship show respect. Is there a lot of unresolved anger. Is there healthy independence. These patterns often show up later in romantic relationships.

Your beliefs matter too. He listens to how you see life, faith, morals, and right and wrong. He is not trying to judge you. He is trying to see if the two of you can actually build a life in the same house without constant conflict about values, parenting, and lifestyle.

He notices how you carry yourself. How you dress, how you treat people who cannot do anything for you, and how you move in public all say something about your self-respect and character. These are things he can see early, not years later.

When intimacy becomes part of the relationship, he pays attention to more than just attraction. He notices whether there is connection, openness, and willingness to grow together. He notices if intimacy feels warm and mutual, or if it becomes distant or disconnected. Sexual compatibility is not everything, but it does matter, and an intentional man does not pretend it does not.

The big difference is this. He is not just collecting these observations and drifting along. He is forming an opinion. He is deciding if the core pieces are already there to build something real. Marriage is built on everyday patterns, not on fantasy or potential.

That is why men who actually want marriage often know within months if a woman is someone they want to build with. Not because they have seen every possible version of her, but because they are looking at the basics. They are not waiting to see every crisis. They are asking, *"Does this person have the character and habits to walk through life with me when life changes?"* Because life will change.

Men who do not know what they want date differently. They go with the flow. They enjoy the connection. They hope something clicks one day. Men who want marriage do not rely on hope. They rely on what they see and then they decide. That is why some relationships move forward and others just keep going in circles.

A man who wants marriage also knows that it goes both ways. It is not just about him deciding if you are wife material. You also get to decide if he is husband material. Because of that, he does not sit back and wait for you to prove yourself. He shows you who he is.

So early on, he shows consistency, care, and stability. He shows you what life with him would actually feel like. He also watches how you respond to that. Some people say they want stability, but when it shows up, it feels uncomfortable because they are used to chaos. An intentional man notices that, not to judge you, but to see if the relationship can grow in a healthy way.

Here is the simple truth that exposes most delayed relationships. If a man does not move like a man who wants a long-term relationship with you, the relationship will not turn into one just because time passes.

YOU CAN'T AUDITION FOR EVERY SEASON

A lot of men say they need to see *"all sides"* of a woman before they decide if they want to build a future with her. They say they need to see her when she is happy, stressed, angry, broke, successful, calm, and under pressure. On the surface, that can sound responsible, like he is being careful. In real life, it often turns into an excuse that gives him unlimited time. The relationship turns into a long audition that never ends, where you are always being evaluated but never chosen.

The truth is, you cannot see every version of a person on command. Life does not work like that. You can date someone for years and still not see how grief changes them until someone close to them dies. You can be with someone for a long time and never see how serious illness changes them until it actually happens. You will not see how infertility, postpartum depression, or major hormonal changes affect a woman until those seasons arrive. Some of the hardest chapters in life do not show up when it is convenient. They show up when they want to.

So when a man says he needs to see every season of you before he decides, what is he really saying. Is he saying he needs to watch you go through every possible hardship before he can choose you, or is he using the idea of "seasons" as a nice-sounding way to avoid choosing at all. At some point, waiting to see everything becomes a way to never decide anything.

A man who actually wants a long-term relationship with you does not need you to prove yourself in every crisis imaginable. He is not looking for perfection. He is looking for basics. He pays attention to how you handle normal stress, everyday responsibility, and regular life problems. He watches how you communicate when things are uncomfortable. He notices how you deal with conflict, whether you can take accountability, and whether you know how to repair issues instead of letting them drag on. Those everyday habits are what shape a real life together far more than rare, dramatic situations.

This is also where *"I need more time"* can be misleading. A lot of the time, a man is not asking for more time to learn who you are. He already knows you well enough. He is asking for more time to enjoy the relationship without having to decide what he is actually building with you.

Waiting longer does not guarantee a better marriage. It does not guarantee you will avoid divorce. People can wait years and still choose the wrong partner. Other people can marry quickly and build a strong life together. Time by itself does not magically create maturity, loyalty, or the ability to build. What matters more is whether both people know what they are building and are actually moving in that direction together, instead of just dating until someone gets tired of waiting.

When a man says, *"I need to see all your seasons,"* pay attention to what that puts on you. It puts you in a position where you are always trying to prove yourself, while he stays free to stay undecided for as long as he wants. It turns marriage into something you have to earn by lasting long enough, instead of something he chooses because he sees a solid foundation with you.

Marriage is not an agreement that you will never change. Everyone changes. Marriage is an agreement that when change happens, you face it together. The real question is not whether life will get hard, that's a given. It is whether you are dealing with a man who chooses relationships on purpose, or a man who keeps one foot out the door while enjoying the comfort of you staying.

If he cannot explain what he is actually waiting to see, then waiting longer will not suddenly help him decide. And if there is no clear moment where he plans to decide, then the waiting itself becomes the relationship. You are no longer building toward something. You are just maintaining a situation.

Two simple actions can help you stay grounded in reality.

First, ask a direct question that brings his criteria into the open. Ask him what he would need to see or experience to feel confident building a long-term relationship with you, and what would tell him that the two of you are not aligned. If he cannot answer that without getting defensive or irritated, that tells you a lot.

Second, watch what actually changes, not what he says. Over the next few months, look for signs that he is building something with you, not just bonding with you. Building shows up in shared planning, shared decisions, and the relationship becoming more defined. If the emotional bond keeps growing but the structure of the relationship never changes, you are not watching someone decide. You are watching someone delay.

When a relationship is moving from girlfriend to fiancée, real parts of his life start to rearrange around you, not just his feelings. This looks like him making decisions that bind his future to yours in practical ways. He starts planning where you both will live instead of just inviting you over. He talks about moving in together with a purpose, not just convenience. He brings up fixing credit so buying a home together is possible one day. He includes you in financial planning, not just asking opinions, but talking about how bills, savings, and long-term goals would work as a unit. He starts thinking in terms of "we" when it comes to location, work moves, and life logistics. You see him making choices that limit his flexibility because he is choosing stability with you. Family starts being treated as shared future family, not just his. His time gets organized around building something, not just fitting you into open spaces. If his life still looks exactly the same as it did when you were just dating, same habits, same priorities, same level of independence, same lack of planning beyond the next few weeks, then the emotional bond may be growing, but the relationship itself is not being built forward.

LOVE AT FIRST SIGHT

Most people have heard the phrase *love at first sight*. The idea has been around for centuries, long before psychology or dating apps existed. Writers and poets used it to describe that instant feeling of recognition or emotional pull when meeting someone for the first time. Over time, the phrase turned into a romantic idea that suggests real love should feel immediate, powerful, and obvious from the start.

In real life, what people often call love at first sight is usually attraction mixed with emotional openness. Attraction can happen to anyone at any time. Emotional openness only happens when a person is actually ready for love. From a man's point of view, the difference matters. A man who is emotionally closed off, unsure about what he wants, or focused on short-term relationships can meet an amazing woman and still not feel anything deep. Not because she is lacking, but because he is not open to experiencing love in the first place.

When a man is genuinely prepared for a long-term relationship, he experiences women differently. He is not just noticing who he is attracted to. He is noticing who he can imagine building a life with. That is when something like love at first sight can happen. It is not magic. It is readiness meeting compatibility. The feeling comes early because the man is already in a mindset where love is allowed to enter. He is not blocking himself emotionally or treating relationships as temporary.

This is where many men get confused, and where many women end up hurt.

A lot of men carry the idea that they are supposed to feel a strong, instant signal that tells them, *"This is the woman I should marry."* They believe that if the feeling is real, it should show up quickly. Because of that belief, some men stay in relationships with women they enjoy, care about, and feel comfortable with, but never fully choose. In the back of their minds, they are waiting for a different feeling. They are waiting for a moment with someone else that feels more dramatic, more intense, or more obvious. Since they did not feel that instant pull early on with the woman they are dating, they quietly assume she is probably not the one.

Instead of being honest about that internal belief, they go through the motions of a relationship. They enjoy the companionship. They enjoy the emotional support. They enjoy the consistency. But they never shift into choosing a long-term relationship with her because they are still holding space for a fantasy moment that may or may not ever happen. The relationship becomes something they stay in, not something they are build in.

This way of thinking creates long waiting periods that feel confusing to the woman. From her side, the relationship may feel real. Time is passing. The connection is deepening. But from his side, he is still mentally open to someone else because he believes the "real" feeling is supposed to be instant and unmistakable. He mistakes the absence of a dramatic early feeling for proof that the relationship is not meant to become long-term, even if the foundation is actually strong.

The truth is, instant emotional certainty is not a reliable way to choose a life partner. Some people do feel a strong connection early and build healthy marriages from it. Others grow into love over time through shared values, compatible direction, and mutual effort. Both paths can work. The difference is not how fast the feeling shows up. The difference is whether a man is emotionally ready to choose someone and build with them, or whether he is using the idea of instant love as a reason to stay undecided.

A man who is prepared for a long-term relationship does not sit in relationships waiting to be emotionally struck by lightning. He pays attention to the foundation in front of him. He looks at character, habits, values, and whether the two of you can actually move through life together. If those pieces are there, he allows himself to choose. If they are not, he does not stay and create false hope.

When a man keeps waiting for a feeling that he thinks should have shown up by now, what he is really doing is avoiding choosing the woman he is already with. The relationship becomes a placeholder. Not because she is lacking, but because he is waiting for a fantasy version of love instead of making a real decision about the relationship he is actually in.

This is why speed alone is not the issue. Some relationships move forward quickly because both people are ready and aligned. Other relationships move slowly because one person is waiting for a feeling to strike them to move forward. The question is not how fast love shows up. The real question is whether the man you are with is emotionally ready to choose a long-term relationship with you, or whether he is staying while quietly waiting for something else or someone else to make him feel certain.

When a man wants a long-term relationship with you, he does not need a perfect emotional moment to choose you. He looks at what is real, what is consistent, and what is possible to build. When he does not want that future with you, no amount of time or emotional closeness will create the feeling he is waiting for.

WAITING FOR THE PERFECT MOMENT

Some men are not waiting for another woman. They are waiting for the perfect moment.

They believe that one day they will suddenly feel fully ready to move forward. They expect a clear internal signal that tells them it is time to commit. Until that moment arrives, they stay where they are. The relationship continues. The time passes. Nothing actually changes.

This way of thinking shows up in other areas of life too. People say they are waiting for the perfect time to start working out, start saving money, change careers, or fix their habits. The truth is simple. The perfect time to start is today. People who wait for perfect conditions usually stay stuck in preparation mode. Life keeps moving, but they stay in the same place.

Some men bring that same mindset into relationships. They are not rejecting the woman they are with. They are postponing a decision because they are waiting to feel more prepared, more stable, or just more certain. They tell themselves that once work slows down, money improves, stress decreases, or life feels more settled, then they will move forward. The problem is that life rarely becomes fully settled. There is always another reason to wait.

This creates confusion for the woman. From her side, the relationship feels real. Time is being invested. The bond is growing. From his side, he is not choosing to move forward. He is waiting for a feeling that may never come. A man who is not ready for a long-term relationship will not feel "that feeling" with anyone, no matter how compatible she is.

Long-term relationships are built through choice, not perfect emotional timing. A man who truly wants a long-term relationship does not wait for life to feel ideal. He decides to move forward when the foundation is already there.

DATING BY THE NUMBERS

These numbers are not rules for your life. They are reference points. They show what most couples who actually move toward marriage tend to do, so you can compare your situation to what is typical instead of guessing whether your timeline is normal or not.

When people are dating with real intention, most of them do not stay in undefined relationships for many years before moving forward. Large surveys of couples in the United States show a pretty consistent pattern.

How long couples date before engagement

- Median dating time before engagement is about 2.5 to 3.5 years
- About 30 percent of couples get engaged within 2 years
- About 53 percent of couples get engaged between 2 and 5 years
- About 17 percent of couples date 6 years or longer before engagement

This shows that most couples who plan to marry spend a few years getting to know each other, then make a decision. Long open ended waiting is not the common path for couples who are actually choosing each other.

How long engagements usually last

- Average engagement length is about 15 months
- The majority of couples get married within 12 to 18 months after engagement

Engagement is usually not treated like a trial period that drags on for years. When people get engaged, they are usually already in motion toward building a life together.

Average age of first-time marriage

- Men average about 30 years old
- Women average about 28 years old

People are marrying later than previous generations, but that does not mean they are staying in long undefined relationships forever. The later age reflects education, career building, and financial stability, not endless dating with no direction.

What long-waiting without movement usually looks like compared to the norm

- Being together 4 to 6 years with no engagement plan is outside the common pattern
- Being together 7 years or more with no clear direction is rare among couples who eventually marry
- Emotional closeness without structural change is more common in relationships that stall

These numbers do not tell you what you should do. They help you see what most people who end up married actually do. If your relationship looks very different from these patterns, the issue is not that you are behind someone else's timeline. The issue is that your relationship is not moving in the direction that most building relationships move.

Time alone does not mean you are getting closer to marriage. Movement does.

8

Is He a Husband?

WHERE HIS VIEW OF MARRIAGE COMES FROM

Some men get into serious relationships without actually wanting a long-term relationship with the woman they are with. They may care about her. They may enjoy her company, the intimacy, and the emotional support she provides. But building a future with her is not what they are thinking about. To him, the relationship fits into his life as something that feels good right now. To her, the relationship feels like it is leading somewhere. The relationship is real to both people, but it does not mean the same thing to both people.

Sometimes men end up in relationships because it feels easier than being alone. When he says he is not ready for something serious, he may stay anyway because staying is easier than ending it and dealing with her tears. But over time this can turn into quiet frustration. A man who feels like he went along with a relationship he did not truly want can later resent the woman, even though he had the ability to walk away the entire time. Relationships that start this way are built on convenience instead of choice, and convenience does not create a strong foundation for marriage.

How a man treats dating is usually how he will treat marriage. If he moves through relationships casually, avoids having real conversations about the future, and never takes ownership of where the relationship is going, he is showing you how he approaches long-term partnership in general. It is not that marriage will magically change him. The way he dates is the preview of how he will approach being a husband. Patterns matter more than promises, because patterns show you how someone actually lives.

A man's early environment often shapes how he views long-term relationships. If he grew up in a home where marriage was not present, not stable, or not taken seriously, marriage may not feel important to him. It may not feel like something people do naturally. He may see long-term relationships as optional because he grew up watching people get by without them. This does not mean he cannot become a good husband. It means that marriage may not feel emotionally necessary to him in the same way it does to someone who grew up seeing it modeled every day.

On the other hand, men who grow up watching two people build a life together often see marriage as a normal part of adulthood. They are used to the idea that relationships involve commitment, sacrifice, and long-term effort. That early example does not guarantee someone will become a good husband, but it does make commitment feel familiar instead of foreign. What feels normal to a person usually feels safer than what feels unfamiliar.

Some men who grew up without fathers respond in very different ways. Some repeat what they saw and do not see long-term commitment as important. Others decide they want the opposite of what they experienced and talk about wanting marriage and family. They don't want to walk in their father's footsteps by giving their child what their father gave them. Wanting something different does not automatically mean being emotionally ready for it. If the motivation comes from anger, hurt, or unresolved pain, those emotions can show up later inside the relationship. The reason someone wants marriage matters, not just the fact that they say they want it.

Change does not happen automatically. A man has to look at how his past shaped him and decide what kind of partner he wants to be on purpose. If he never reflects on how his upbringing affected him, he will likely repeat the same patterns he grew up around, even if he swears he will not. What people grow up with often becomes what feels normal, even when it is unhealthy.

This is not about blaming childhood for adult choices. It is about understanding that early experiences shape what feels normal in relationships. If a man grew up around unstable relationships, instability may feel familiar to him. Growth means questioning what feels normal and choosing to build something healthier than what you were shown.

As a woman, it is not your job to fix a man's past or teach him how to become a husband. You cannot heal his childhood. You cannot do his emotional work for him. What you can do is pay attention to patterns. You can listen to how he talks about his parents, his upbringing, and his past relationships. You can notice whether he takes responsibility for his growth or avoids it. But the decision to become a different man has to come from him.

A man who is actually ready for marriage is not just choosing a woman. He is choosing to live differently. He is choosing to build a life instead of drifting through relationships. He is choosing to stop repeating what feels familiar when what feels familiar has not led to healthy relationships. That choice has to be internal. No woman can make it for him.

HAS HE SHOWN YOU HUSBAND-TRAITS?

Many women spend years trying to figure out why a man has not taken the next step. They assume the missing piece is time, reassurance, safety, or the right moment. They believe that if the relationship feels good enough, deep enough, or stable enough, it will eventually turn into marriage. What often goes unexamined is whether the man in front of them has ever actually **shown** that he wants to be a husband in the first place. Marriage does not usually appear out of nowhere at the end of a long relationship. It grows out of how a man has already been showing up all along.

A man does not become a husband just because enough time has passed. Time does not change his direction. A man becomes a husband because he decides to live like a man who is building a future with one woman. If that way of living has never shown up in his behavior, waiting longer does not create it.

This is where the focus has to shift. Up to this point, the attention has been on noticing delays, understanding comfort, and seeing how relationships stall. Now the focus turns to evaluation. Not evaluation based on chemistry, potential, or emotional attachment, but evaluation based on behavior. How has this man actually lived inside the relationship. Has he moved like someone building a future with you, or like someone enjoying a relationship that fits neatly into his current life.

A husband is not defined by charm, money, looks, or sexual chemistry. Those things can create attraction and attachment, but they do not build a life. A man who wants a long-term relationship shows it in how he thinks beyond himself, how he includes you in real life decisions, and how he moves with purpose instead of drifting. He does not treat the relationship like something that exists only in the present moment. He moves like someone who understands that choosing a woman also means showing up for her future, not just enjoying her present.

If a man has never shown any concern for building a shared life with you, then marriage is not being delayed. It is not what he is aiming for with you. Waiting does not turn a casual approach into a committed one. It only makes the waiting longer.

Many women stay emotionally committed to men who are good partners in the moment but have never shown long-term thinking. The relationship can feel loving, consistent, and familiar, which makes it harder to see what is missing. But feeling comfortable with someone is not the same as watching them build a future with you. A man can enjoy companionship, affection, and routine without wanting a lifelong partnership. When that happens, the woman often ends up waiting for a version of him that has never actually shown up in real life.

This chapter is not about blaming or shaming anyone. It is about seeing clearly. It is about separating who a man has shown himself to be from who you hope he will become.

Wanting a husband does not turn the man you are with into someone who wants a long-term relationship with you.

As hard as that realization can be, it can also be freeing. When you stop asking why he hasn't married you, you can start asking whether he has ever shown you that building a life with you was something he wanted to do at all. That shift changes how you see the relationship, because it moves you out of waiting for potential and into paying attention to the reality he's presenting. And you realize that it's not about proving your worth to him, it's about asking yourself if he is deserving of a wife such as yourself. Does he deserve you forever?

HUSBAND BEHAVIOR IS NOT A MYSTERY

One of the biggest lies in dating is the idea that it takes years to figure out if a man is the type who wants to be your husband. Men who want that are not hiding it. You do not need endless time, endless patience, or emotional endurance to figure them out. What a man wants always shows up in how he moves.

A man who sees himself building a future with one woman does not treat dating like something casual. He is not just passing time or seeing how things feel. Early on, he is paying attention to whether the two of you make sense long-term. At the same time, he is not sitting back watching you prove yourself forever. He understands that choosing each other goes both ways, so he also shows up in a way that lets you see what life with him would actually feel like.

This is where a lot of women misread the situation. Because a man is present, affectionate, or consistent, it is easy to assume he is moving toward marriage in his own time. But being present is not the same as wanting a long-term relationship with you. A man can show up regularly and still have no plans to build a future with you. Being around is easy. Choosing a future with someone is not.

A man who wants a long-term relationship with you takes direction seriously. He does not avoid talking about where things are going. He does not keep everything loose so he can stay comfortable. He is clear about what he wants and where he sees things going. Not because he is trying to pressure you, but because he respects your time and your emotions. He does not keep you guessing about the future while enjoying the benefits of you staying.

His care also looks different. It is not random or only when it is convenient. He checks on you because he cares about how you are actually doing, not because he is trying to smooth something over. He follows through because being dependable matters to him, not because he is afraid you will get upset. Over time, his actions line up with his words without you having to carry the emotional weight of reminding him who he said he would be.

A man who wants to be your husband does not shy away from building real life plans. **Talking about money, living situations, or future goals does not scare him off. It pulls him in.** He does not want intimacy without structure. He does not want a relationship that only works as long as nothing becomes serious. If he wants you long-term, he is willing to let the relationship become real in real life ways.

When those patterns are missing, it is usually not because the relationship needs more time. It is because the man does not want a long-term relationship with you.

A lot of women wait for a man to become someone he has never shown himself to be. They hope comfort will turn into leadership and that affection will turn into direction. Men do not drift into wanting marriage. That is a decision they make internally, and their behavior reflects it long before any proposal happens.

If a man has never shown you that he wants a long-term relationship with you, then marriage is not being delayed. It is not what he is moving toward with you. Waiting does not change that.

THE QUESTION THAT CHANGES EVERYTHING

After all the explanations, patterns, and examples in this book, the most important shift comes down to one simple question. It is not the question most women start with, and it is not the one people usually encourage you to ask.

The question is not, *"Why hasn't he made me his wife?"*
The real question is, *"Has he truly ever **shown** me that he wants to be my husband?"*

That question changes everything because it takes hope and waiting out of the picture and replaces them with what you can actually see. It stops you from waiting on a man to become something and forces you to look at what he has already shown you through how he lives and how he treats you.

A lot of women spend years trying to earn marriage from men who have never shown that they want a long-term relationship. They believe that if they love harder, stay longer, or become more understanding, the man will eventually decide to build a life with them. But marriage does not come from lasting long in a situation. It comes from a man already wanting to build something real with you.

A man does not become a husband just because he proposes. He shows you he wants to build a life with you by how he moves long before any ring shows up.

A man who wants a long-term relationship with you shows steady care. He does not emotionally check out when things get uncomfortable. He does not enjoy the benefits of being with you while avoiding building anything real with you. He does not treat talking about the future like pressure or treat commitment like a trap. He understands that building a life together means making choices, giving things up, and leading with intention, and he does not avoid that.

When those things are missing, that matters more than the fact that he is affectionate sometimes.

Sometimes the reason a man has not married you has very little to do with you. It has more to do with the fact that he does not see himself as your husband or as a husband in general. He may enjoy your company. He may like being with you. He may enjoy the comfort of the relationship. But liking you and enjoying you is not the same as choosing to build a life with you.

Men do not move into marriage just because time passes. They move into marriage because they decide to build a life with someone.

If a man has never talked about building a future with you, never included you in real life planning, never treated your future as something he is responsible for, and never moved in ways that show he is building toward something permanent with you, then the lack of a ring is not confusing. It is consistent with how he has been living.

The real danger is not ending up with the wrong man. The real danger is staying with a man whose behavior you already understand, but continuing to explain it away with hope. Waiting longer does not change what a man has already shown you. Paying attention sooner does.

When you change the question from *"Why hasn't he made me his wife?"* to *"Has he truly ever* ***shown*** *me that he wants to be my husband?"* you stop negotiating with time and stop holding onto potential. You start making decisions based on what is actually happening.

Two practical actions you can take from this chapter are these.

First, write down five specific behaviors you personally need from a man who wants a long-term relationship with you, in plain language. Next to each one, write one real example of when he has clearly shown that behavior in the last six months. If you can't think of any examples, that speaks for itself.

Second, have one honest conversation that focuses on what he is actually doing, not just how he feels. Let him know you are paying attention to whether the relationship is moving toward something more serious, and ask him what steps he believes you two can implement to move it forward. Then pay attention to what actually changes over the next 30 to 60 days, not just what he says in that moment.

A man who sees himself building a life with you naturally starts thinking in terms of “we” instead of “me.” He talks about where the two of you will live, the investments the two of you will make, and how the two of you will raise your children. He speaks in terms of togetherness. This is a man who is building a clear mental picture of a future with you.

CLOSING:

If there is one truth this book has returned to again and again, it is this. Time does not create clarity. Comfort does not create commitment. Love alone does not create direction. What shapes a future is choice, followed by action.

Most women are not confused because they lack intelligence or discernment. They are confused because hope is powerful, attachment is real, and patience can feel like maturity. When you care deeply, your heart naturally searches for reasons to stay optimistic. You give the benefit of the doubt. You wait for things to settle. You trust that effort will eventually be rewarded. None of that makes you naive. It makes you human.

But clarity requires a different posture than hope. Clarity asks you to observe what is actually happening, not what you wish would happen. It asks you to notice patterns instead of isolated moments. It asks you to evaluate behavior instead of interpreting emotion. And most of all, it asks you to respect your own time as something valuable, not something to be negotiated away quietly.

A relationship should not require you to shrink your expectations in order to survive inside it. It should not ask you to live in constant uncertainty while offering just enough comfort to keep you steady. It should not train you to silence your own needs in the name of peace. Healthy connection does not depend on endurance. It grows through alignment, shared direction, and mutual responsibility.

You do not need to prove that you are worthy of commitment. You do not need to wait long enough, love hard enough, or adjust yourself enough to earn clarity. The right relationship will not make you question whether you are moving forward. You will feel the forward motion in how decisions are made, how plans are formed, and how responsibility is shared.

Sometimes the bravest thing you can do is stop interpreting and start accepting. Accept what someone is showing you. Accept what is not changing. Accept what continues to remain undefined. Acceptance is not bitterness. It is honesty.

Choosing clarity does not always mean walking away immediately. Sometimes it means slowing your investment until direction exists. Sometimes it means asking better questions and listening carefully to the answers. Sometimes it means giving yourself permission to want a relationship that is built intentionally, not accidentally. And sometimes it means releasing what feels familiar in order to make room for what is aligned.

You are allowed to want certainty. You are allowed to want leadership, effort, and consistency. You are allowed to want a partner who sees building a life as a responsibility, not a burden. Those desires are not too much. They are reasonable.

If this book has done its job, it has not told you what decision to make. It has helped you see more clearly how decisions are revealed. It has helped you understand what delay really looks like, what intention actually feels like, and why comfort can quietly replace growth if you are not paying attention.

The goal is not to fear relationships. The goal is to choose them wisely. Your time matters. Your peace matters. Your future matters.

And clarity, when you allow yourself to stand in it fully, will always lead you toward what truly belongs with you.

E STILL

RESTING IN THE SEASON YOU'RE IN

Sometimes when you feel uncertain, confused, or emotionally tired, your instinct is to start searching for answers. You begin asking God what your next move should be, which direction to go, what decision to make, and what needs to change. You wait for a clear sign, a push, or a moment that tells you what to do next. And when that answer does not come quickly, anxiety begins to creep in. You start to feel like you are behind, like you should be doing something more, like there is a problem that needs to be solved. But sometimes the message is not to move at all. Sometimes the message is simply to be still.

There are seasons in life that are not broken, even if they feel quiet, slow, or unfamiliar. Not every season is meant to be fixed, rushed through, or escaped. Some seasons exist to teach you how to rest inside your own life instead of constantly trying to outrun it. Many women spend their lives chasing the next version of themselves, the next relationship, the next level, the next breakthrough, or the next chapter. And while growth is beautiful, there is also something sacred about learning how to live fully inside the season you are already in.

Sometimes God places you exactly where you are, not to frustrate you, but to steady you. He does this to calm your nervous system, soften your heart, slow your thinking, teach you how to trust without needing constant reassurance, and show you that your peace does not have to depend on what changes next. There is a difference between waiting with anxiety and waiting with peace. One keeps you restless and unsettled, while the other allows you to breathe, enjoy your days, and trust that what is meant for you does not require panic to arrive.

This matters deeply for women when it comes to love and relationships. When your heart starts racing ahead of your life, you can begin making decisions from pressure instead of clarity. You may start forcing timelines, chasing validation, or attaching yourself to situations that feel emotionally safe but are not aligned spiritually or practically. Stillness protects you from that. It teaches you how to hear yourself again, how to enjoy your own presence, how to stop negotiating your peace for potential, and how to trust timing without needing control.

Being still does not mean giving up on love, lowering your standards, or shrinking your desires. It means you stop letting fear drive your decisions. It means you allow your life to breathe. It means you trust that if something is meant to move, it will move without you having to force it. **Some seasons are meant to be lived, not solved.** Some seasons are meant to be enjoyed, not rushed. Some seasons are meant to strengthen your inner world so that when your next chapter arrives, you step into it grounded, clear, and emotionally steady rather than anxious, rushed, or depleted.

If you are in a quiet season right now, let it be quiet. If your life feels simple right now, let it be simple. If things feel stable right now, let them be stable. Not every chapter needs drama to be meaningful, and not every season needs urgency to be productive.

Sometimes the greatest growth happens when nothing on the outside looks like it is changing at all.

Letting God carry your stress does not require you to fix anything or figure anything out. Be still. If you are trying to figure out what to do next, the answer may be to do nothing at all. This book was meant to bring clarity instead of pressure, awareness instead of anxiety, and discernment instead of fear. Whether your next step is to walk away from something, rebuild something, or simply rest where you are, let that decision come from peace instead of panic.

You are not behind. You are not late. You are not missing what is meant for you. Sometimes the most powerful thing you can do is stop trying to fix what God has already placed you in and simply learn how to live well inside it.

Be still.

CONTINUE THE CONVERSATION WITH ME

This book was never meant to be the end of the conversation. It was meant to start one.

Every relationship has its own details, history, emotions, and decisions that cannot always be fully addressed inside a book. Sometimes clarity comes from being able to talk through what you are actually experiencing, not just what you read on the page.

If you have a relationship question, a situation you want perspective on, or something this book stirred up that you would like to unpack, my email is open for personal one-on-one questions.

By scanning the QR code below, you can submit your question and leave your email anonymously so I can respond directly. This gives you a private space to ask honestly, get grounded feedback, and think through your next steps with clarity instead of confusion.

Whether you are dating, waiting, deciding, healing, or simply trying to understand what you are seeing in your relationship, your question matters. Sometimes one clear conversation can shift how you see everything.

I look forward to hearing from you.

Proverbs 31:10

"Who can find a virtuous woman? For her worth is far above rubies."

"It's not about the amount of time you two spend together. It's about the quality conversations you have together. You both gossip and have a laugh, great! But is that conversation building your future? Make sure you have more future-building conversations. I don't mean talks about marriage but instead talks about those foundational pillars that the marriage will stand on. Some people never have those discussions. As a result, they never learn who they're building with. They just know that the person currently makes them happy. Happiness is great...but when the ground starts to shake, and the smiles disappear.... what will you two be standing on?"

-Manuel V. Johnson

www.ingramcontent.com/pod-product-compliance
Lightning Source LLC
LaVergne TN
LVHW090614110826
845146LV00001B/385

9798993863818